# YOUR KNOWLEDGE HAS VALUE

**Bibliographic information published by the German National Library:**

The German National Library lists this publication in the National Bibliography; detailed bibliographic data are available on the Internet at http://dnb.dnb.de .

**Imprint:**

Copyright © 2019 GRIN Verlag
Print and binding: Books on Demand GmbH, Norderstedt Germany
ISBN: 9783346098658

**This book at GRIN:**

https://www.grin.com/document/511977

**Biruk Chemere**

# The History of Coffee Production in Brazil and Ethiopia. A Comparative Overview

GRIN Verlag

**GRIN - Your knowledge has value**

Since its foundation in 1998, GRIN has specialized in publishing academic texts by students, college teachers and other academics as e-book and printed book. The website www.grin.com is an ideal platform for presenting term papers, final papers, scientific essays, dissertations and specialist books.

**Visit us on the internet:**

http://www.grin.com/

http://www.facebook.com/grincom

http://www.twitter.com/grin_com

# The History of Coffee Production in Brazil and Ethiopia. A Comparative Study

## Abstract

Coffee produced and consumed internationally, and this popular crop produced mainly in tropical regions. Developed countries are the main consumers of this crop. It is also the leading exporting item for some countries like Ethiopia. However, in Brazil due to the diversification of products, coffee did not take the forefront of leading export items. The coffee production industry of Brazil is well productive unlike Ethiopia's. This article will discuss the production of coffee in both countries. In the first section, it will discuss coffee production history of Brazil and in the second section it will discuss coffee production in Ethiopia, and finally, it will compare coffee production in both countries and put some suggestions for the good being of production of coffee in Ethiopia.

Keywords

*Coffea arabica,* Forest Coffee Production, Semi – Forest Coffee Production, Garden Coffee Production, Plantation Coffee Production

Author

Biruk Wondimu Chemere, Raya University, Department of History and Heritage Management;

# Table of contents

# Coffee

Coffee is one of the high – priced crop and the second widely traded commodity in the world next to oil (Clarke, Macrae, 1989a and Watt, 1937). It is produced and consumed globally, and millions of Peoples depend on it either directly or indirectly. In addition, the trees of coffee belong to botanical *genus Coffea* in the family *Rubiaceae* (Clarke, Macrae, 1988b). Like other crops, the productivity of coffee per tree varied based on the condition of climate and Soil, the cultivation system as well as the age of the tree. It was during the last decades of the nineteenth century, that coffee became widely consumed all over the world (Revels, 2000).

Coffee growth in favorably temperature ranging from 15 – 24 °C, and with the annual rainfall between 1500 – 2000 mm, but if the temperature gets higher than 24 °C the occurrence of photosynthesis will be low and the leaf and production will be damage (Clarke, Macrae, 1988 b). In some areas, the rainfall reduced until 1000 mm, but they used irrigation as sustenance. Volcanic soil with high Base Exchange is favorable soil type for Coffee production, but it is also possible to plant Coffee with soil types like sandstone, limestone, basalt, and lava (Clarke, Macrae, 1988 b).

## Coffee Production in Brazil

Federative Republic of Brazil located in the eastern part of South America, in the Western Hemisphere. Nine countries and one French Overseas territory shared a border with Brazil;Chile and Ecuador are the only two South American countries that did not share any boundary with Brazil. The climate condition of Brazil varies from hot and humid in the Amazon Rainforest, to temperate in the south. The northeast suffers periodic droughts while heavy rains cause severe damage in the south, especially in poorer areas of the cities (Motta and Hargrave, et al, 2011). Brazil's population is around 195 million and its official language is Portuguese.

*Coffea arabica* introduced to Latin America from Ethiopia in the first decades of the eighteenth century (Clarke, Macrae, 1988b and Walson, 2008). However, it does not mean that other coffee species like Robusta originated from Latina America. In the last quarter of the eighteenth century, small plantations started in the State of Rio de Janeiro, later on, the plantations spread to the states of São Paulo, Minas Geraes, and Spirito Santo, and by the first quarter of the nineteenth century, those small plantations became the leading force in the agriculture sector of Brazil (*Journal of Royal Society of Arts*, 1913: p. 449). From the last quarter of the nineteenth century to the beginning of the twentieth century, three fourth of world coffee production and two-third of Brazil's coffee production came from the State of São Paulo (Martin, 1954 and Font, 1987). Therefore, at that time, one state of a country i.e. the state of São Paulo produced approximately half of the world's coffee production. Even if it looks exaggerations, some authors tried to describe the high productivity of coffee in São Paulo from those, ''São Paulo is the coffee state and Santos the coffee port of the World'' (Sawyer, 1907) and ''No other country shows such a vast areas planted in coffee as does São Paulo, and in no other country is the production per acre equal to that yielded by the plantation of this state'' (*Journal of Royal Society of Arts*, 1913: p. 450) were fascinating expressed.

Within approximately a century, the production and export of coffee in Brazil shown great development. The next table will show clear statistics about the growth of coffee export c. nineteenth century.

| Year of exportation | Amount of exported in a pound |
|---------------------|-------------------------------|
| 1800 | 1,720,000 |
| 1830 | 64,000,000 |
| 1840 | 137,000,000 |
| 1907 | 2,000,000,000 |
| 1909 | 2,233,000,000 |

Table 1. Source: the Production of Coffee in Brazil in the Journal of Royal Society of Arts, Vol. 61, No. 3146 March 7, 1913, P. 451.

In the first decades of the twentieth century, from the industrial workers of Brazil, nearly 93.3% were engaged in the production or transaction of coffee (*Journal of Royal Society of Arts*, 1913: p. 450). In addition, 85% of capitals invested in all industries were engaged in the production or transaction of coffee (*Journal of Royal Society of Arts*, 1913: p. 450). In 1901 failing of coffee price had occurred in Brazil, and overproduction was the reason behind the failure of the price, to

4

control it the legislative of the State if São Paulo discouraged the establishment of new plantation program in the state (Sawyer, 1907). The overproduction of coffee in Brazil could take as one of the yardsticks of the high productivity of coffee in the area and also the attention of the concerning body for the production of the crop. In the first two decades of the second half of the twentieth century, when the then government of Brazil implemented export-oriented economy, coffee farmers have been supported by government subsidies, and state – finance researches patronized ever before (Walson, Achinelli, 2008). In 1985, coffee covers 11 % of total Brazil export revenues with 2.5 billion USD (Clarke, Macrae, 1988b).

## Coffee Production Systems in Brazil

Unlike other coffee-producing countries, especially Ethiopia, the coffee production system in Brazil take place by large government and private farms (Walson, Achinelli, 2008). However, it does not mean that there are no small – scale coffee farmers; the share of small – scale farmers was near to the ground on annual production. In short, when we talk about coffee production system in Brazil, it is all about large scale farms or plantation coffee production systems. The history of large scale coffee production systems in Brazil had a long history as back as the introduction of coffee to the continent in the eighteenth century (Walson, Achinelli, 2008). The large coffee plantations were owned by private and group investors, and they played a great role in the improvement of Brazilians coffee production. The Common, plantation was as large as having from 300,000-400,000 coffee trees, and there were plantations with coffee trees of 800,000 in the beginning of the twentieth century (*Journal of Royal Society of Arts*, 1913: p. 450). The next table will show the largeness of Brazil's coffee plantations and their growth in partial.

| Year | Trees per a plantation |
|------|------------------------|
| 1888 | 211,000,000            |
| 1902 | 545,000,000            |
| 1905 | 689,000,000            |

Table 2 Source: the Production of Coffee in Brazil in the Journal of Royal Society of Arts, Vol. 61, No. 3146 March 7, 1913, P. 450.

5

# Coffee Production in Ethiopia

Federal Democratic Republic of Ethiopia located in Northeast Africa, shares a border with Sudan in the west, with South Sudan in the southwest, Kenya in the south, Somalia in southeast and east, Djibouti in the east and Eritrea in the north. The population of the country is around 90 million. Like Brazil, the environment of Ethiopia varies from region to region, when the northern and eastern parts of the country got an average and small amount of rainfall per year respectively, and other parts of the country got a relatively good amount of rainfall per year. The southwestern parts of the country got the highest amount of rainfall than any other parts of the country.

In the world, there are different types of coffee species exist, but in Ethiopia, *Coffea arabica* is the main species produce on vast scale. It is possible to say that there is no exact and popularly accepted answer for the questions where, how, and when the production and consumption of coffee started in Ethiopia (Asfaw, 2014)? Nevertheless, the sentences, "coffee was originated in the southwest of Ethiopia, is relatively inclusive to the dispute over the first place of the discovery of coffee." *Coffea arabica* grew first in the forest highlands of Southwest Ethiopia, with the long rainy season and favorable soil type for the growth of coffee (Clarke, Macrae, 1988b and Kieran, 1969). Then, it spread to the world through the Arabian Peninsula.

Exporting coffee had a long history in Ethiopia, and history goes as back as the seventeenth century. After the second half of the nineteenth century, coffee emerged as one of the important export items, which was largely produced in the Southwestern parts of Ethiopia (Zewde, 2005). As taxation and revenues from trade were the base for the power of the then regional lords of the kingdoms, coffee supported most of the rulers. In the second decade of the twentieth century, coffee became one most important exporting item for the then monarchical leaders, some of the young imperial governors, who had alerted about the revenue from coffee plantation, started their own coffee plantation in the southwest; notably *Dajazmach* Desta Damtew and *Dajazmach* Mekonen Demissew were some of the personality who had started their plantation. Nevertheless, it does not mean that they were the first prominent leader to establish a modern coffee plantation in Ethiopia. Due to the growth of the attention of the government and coffee production, the then modern road from Addis Ababa to Jimma, (which created a link between one of the centers of coffee production and processing town to the capital of the country) completed in the 1930s.

After the above mentioned two phenomena i.e. the establishment of plantation by the imperial governors and the construction of the then-modern road, the contribution of coffee on the national export items got advanced. The next table shows the share of coffee in the export items of the country during the mid-twentieth century.

|  | 1949 | 1950 | 1951 | 1952 | 1953 |
|---|---|---|---|---|---|
| Export of Coffee | 8,900,000 USD | 13,000,000 USD | 25,000,000 USD | 20,100,000 USD | 40,000,000 USD |
| All other export | 19,700,000 USD | 15,300,000 USD | 21,700,000 USD | 21,600,000 USD | 22,000,000 USD |
| Total export | 28,600,000 USD | 28,300,000 USD | 46,700,000 USD | 41,700,000 USD | 62,000,000 USD |

Table 3. ZbigniewSiemienski, ''Impact of the Coffee Boom on Ethiopia.'' *Middle East Journal*, Vol. 9, No. 1, 1955.P. 67.

The production and consumption of Coffee are vital for the cultural and economic value of Ethiopians. The value of coffee was not only economical but also it had great value for the cultural aspects of society. Half of the coffee produced was consumed locally, even in the southwest of the country, there are unique ceremonies of drinking coffee (Asfaw, 2014 and Bastin, Matteucci, 2007). Even if the rank of Ethiopia in the list of top coffee producers country varies from time to time, most of the time it was in the fifth coffee producers in the world and the first producer in Africa. Ethiopians are the heavy coffee drinkers, ranked as one of the largest coffee consumers in sub-Saharan Africa (Asfaw, 2014 and Bastin, Matteucci, 2007 and Report of United States Agency for International Development, June 2010: P. 1).

Oromia and "Southern Nations Nationalities and Peoples'" Regional States are the top coffee producers with 63.3 and 35.9 percent of the nation's production of coffee respectively and the major coffee growing districts Wadarda's contain an estimated 800,000 coffee farmers (Report of United States Agency for International Development, June 2010: P. 2). By the fragmentation of coffee farmlands in major coffee producing regions and absence of a well – organized census, it becomes difficult to put the exact number of coffee producing farmers, but it estimates that they are between 15 - 20 million (Bastin, Matteucci, 2007 and Asfaw, 2014).

## Coffee Production System in Ethiopia

In Ethiopia, the most common types of coffee production systems are forest coffee production, semi – forest coffee production, garden coffee production, and plantation coffee production.

Forest coffee production system is based on wild coffee grown under the shade of natural forest trees and it does not have a definite owner (Report of United States Agency for International Development, June 2010: P. 2). Coffee in the forest is possible to find only in East Africa and *Coffea arabica* as a wild only find in Southwest Ethiopia (Clarke, Macrae, 1988 b). The production of wild coffee started in Ethiopia around the second quarter of the twentieth century. Still, now, they exist in the southwestern parts of Ethiopia. During the harvest time, the population around the forest collected the cherry, but after the harvest time, the management of the farmers to the coffee became low. Moreover, the production of forest coffee is low if we compare to the garden and plantation coffee production system. The low production is the result of poor management that is the descending from communal ownership of the land (Asfaw, 2014).

The production of semi – forest coffee is nearly related to forest coffee production (Report of United States Agency for International Development, June 2010: P. 1). Like the forest coffee production system, the coffee trees grew naturally, but unlike the forest coffee production system, the wild coffee got good management not only in harvest time but also before harvest time. Another difference that semi – forest coffee production systems have with forest coffee production is that in the forest coffee production the coffee tress did not have one definite owner, but here in the semi – forest coffee production there is a farmer who is responsible for the coffee tress. This makes semi – forest coffee production relatively productive than forest coffee production.

Garden coffee production system contributed almost half of Ethiopia's coffee production and it existed before coffee plantations were established. Small – scale coffee farmers in all coffee growing areas included in this garden coffee production system, and coffee cultivated with other cereal crops (Report of United States Agency for International Development, June 2010: P. 1). In this type of coffee production system, the farm normally established near to the farmer's house, and unlike forest and semi – forest coffee production systems, the coffee trees fertilized with organic fertilizers.

The plantation coffee production system is the last to establish in Ethiopia than other types of coffee production systems. It was at the beginning of the twentieth century that coffee plantations had been felt in the history of the coffee production of the country. Even if they got extraordinary support with scientific researches and fertilizers (Report of United States Agency for International Development, June 2010: P. 1), they did not have a great share to the national coffee production like that of the garden coffee production system. Mostly government institutions are owners of the plantation in Ethiopia and created jobs for tens of thousands of peoples (Report of United States Agency for International Development, June 2010: P. 1).

## Comparison of Coffee Production in Brazil and Ethiopia

Thousands of coffee strains are found in Ethiopia, from those strains twenty-four of them are under the varieties of *Coffea arabica*, and also two-third of Ethiopia's coffee classified as specialty coffee (Report of United States Agency for International Development, June 2010: P. 1). In addition, more than half of Ethiopia's coffee is organic. The above things did not only make a difference with Brazil, but it makes Ethiopia a unique country in the coffee production of the globe. The other major thing that makes the difference between Brazil and Ethiopia concerning coffee is the high consumption of coffee by Ethiopians. Ethiopians had the habit of drinking coffee before they export it to other parts of the globe (Pankhurst, 1961), but in Brazil the sequence was revers, first coffee plantations were established for the sought of export to Europe and North America, later, through time coffee became consumed locally. What makes unique the consumption of coffee by Ethiopians is that within the past ten years the consumption increased radically. The emergence of small roadside stalls selling coffee to passers on major towns of the country was behind the growth of coffee consumption locally (Asfaw, 2014). The small stalls serve coffee in a traditional manner. They had emerged and flourished in Ethiopian's major towns very popular among coffee consumers who are irritated by the growing price of coffee served in cafes (Asfaw, 2014). Unlike regular coffee shops, the small stalls pay neither value-added tax (VAT) nor such heavy house rents, which resulted from their cost of serving coffee much lower than the regular coffee shops (Asfaw, 2014).

The volume of production was another thing that makes the difference between Ethiopia's and Brazil's coffee production. Brazil had faced overproduction frequently in its coffee production history, but, inversely Ethiopia had faced underproduction through its coffee production history. Khat is one of the reasons behind Ethiopia's coffee underproduction. Khat (*Catha-edulis*)is the second-largest export item for Ethiopia and competing for cash crop production with coffee and another cash crop in coffee-growing areas (Hailu, Aune, 2003). It is a crop with relatively high resistance to drought, disease, and pests than other crops, and it is possible to harvest throughout the year (Asfaw, 2014 and Hailu, Aune, 2003). The above reasons make Khat less risky to produce than any other crop in Ethiopia to small – scale farmers. Nowadays, due to the above advantages of Khat, most of the coffee farmers shifted their cultivation to khat, mainly in Jimma Zone coffee producing areas and this affected the coffee production of the country on a large scale.

The drafts and implementations of the policies concerning coffee in both governments were very diverse. Starting from the introduction of coffee to Brazil, their government gave high attention to the production of coffee and supported the farmers. In addition, during the first two decades of the second half of the twentieth century, the assistance of the government reached its pick (Walson, Achinelli, 2008). On the other hand, here in Ethiopia, the conditions were inverse, government organization does not have specialized initiations that provide extensive support for coffee production as like coffee supported the economy of the country (Asfaw, 2014). Research centers that work on the improvement of genetics, the ability of coffee seeds to resisted drought and pests was rare (Clarke, Macrae, 1988 b). The occurrence of Coffee Berry Disease (CBD) is high in Ethiopia, which takes approximately half of the production in risk (Report of United States Agency for International Development, June 2010: P. 2). A poor harvest and post-harvest activities highly reduced the quality and quantity of coffee in Ethiopia (Report of United States Agency for International Development, June 2010: P. 3). Even if the government gave a credit to small scale former, it was not as important as the farmers got from informal sources like moneylenders and traders (Hailu, Aune, 2003).

Land and labor are some of the main determinant factors for the productivity of coffee. In the coffee-growing areas of Brazil, two of them found easily and with low price (Kelly Walson, P. 232) unlike Ethiopia, whom in harvest time daily laborers migrated from non-coffee growing areas due to the lack of daily laborer in coffee-growing areas. The coffee-growing areas of Brazil are

10

much nearer to the sea, which is too easy and cheap means of transportation. On the other hand, here in Ethiopia, the main coffee growing areas, i.e. southwest is far from the sea, than that of the Brazilians coffee growing areas. As a result, the above two factors make the coffee of Brazil cheaper than the coffee Ethiopia and rejected the coffee of Ethiopia by the consumers who need a low price of coffee.

Yields of coffee in Ethiopia are very low when we compare to other producing countries mainly with Brazil, with estimates of less than 200 kg per hectare for forest coffee and around 450 – 750kg per hectare for garden coffee with modern systems of cultivation. In addition, Coffee production in Brazil and other producing countries take placed by plantation whether owned by the government or private, but here in Ethiopia, approximately ninety percent of the productions take place by small – scale farmers (Report of United States Agency for International Development, June 2010: P. 2). Unlike Brazilians, in Ethiopia, most farmers did not use fertilizers and pesticides, and also it's difficult to an accurate estimation of coffee production due to some part of the production came from forest and semi – forest areas and also nearly half of the production is consumed locally (Report of United States Agency for International Development, June 2010: P. 2).

# Conclusion

What I understand from the coffee production of Ethiopia is that the government and the stakeholders of coffee production in Ethiopia should have to learn a lot from the Brazilians. The government of Ethiopia did not give attention and assistance to the vast small coffee producers of the country as they had a great role in the country's export role. The production of the country should improve both in quality and quantity due to the production's great interest in the market than any other coffee-producing countries.

# References

Alemayehu Asfaw. (2014) Coffee Production and Marketing in Ethiopia. *European Journal of Business and Management* 6 (37): 109 – 121.

Bahiru Zewde. (2005) *A Short History of Modern Ethiopia; 1855-1991*. Oxford, Athens, Addis Ababa: Oxford University Press

(1909) Brazil's Failure to Control the Price of Coffee. *Bulletin of the American Geographical Society* 41 (4)

Clarke, R.J, R. Macrae. (1989) *Coffee; Chemistry*. Vol. I. New York

Clarke, R.J, R. Macrae. (1988) *Coffee; Agronomy*. Vol. IV. New York

Da Motta, Ronaldo, Jorge Hargrave, Gustavo Luedemann, et al. (2011) *Climate Change in Brazil; Economic, social, and regulatory aspects*. Brasilia.

(2010) *Ethiopian Coffee Industry Value Chain Analysis*. Report of the United States Agency for International Development, June.

Font, Mauricio A. (1987) Coffee Planters, Politics, and Development in Brazil. *Latin American Research Review* 22 (3): 136 – 142.

Guluma Gemeda. (2002) The Rise of Coffee and the Demise of Colonial Autonomy; The Oromo Kingdom of Jimma and Political Centralization. *Northeast African Studies* 9 (3): 51 – 74

Kieran, J.A. (1969) The Origin of Commercial Arabica Coffee Production in East Africa. *AfricanHistorical Studies* 2 (1): 51 – 67.

Martin, Frances H. (1954) A History of Coffee Price in the United States; 1840-1954. *Monthly Labor Review* 77 (7): 765 – 767.

Pankhurst, Richard. (1961) *An Introduction to the Economic History of Ethiopia; from Early times to 1800*. London.

Revels, S. Craig. (2000) Coffee in Nicaragua; Introduction and Expansion in the nineteenth century. *Conference of Latin Americanist Geographers* 26: 17 – 28.

Sawyer, Frederic H. (1907) Coffee production in São Paulo, Brazil. *The Geographical Journal.* 29 (3): 353 – 354.

Siemienski, Zbigniew. (1955) Impact of the Coffee Boom on Ethiopia. *Middle East Journal.* 9 (1): 67 – 75

Taye Hailu, Jens B. Aune. (2003) Khat Expansion in the Ethiopian Highland; Effects on the Farming System in Harbo District. *Mountain Research and Development*. 23 (2): 185 –189

(1913) The Production of Coffee in Brazil. *Journal of Royal Society of Arts*. 61 (3146): 427 – 456

Walson, Kelly, Moria L. Achinelli (2008) Context and Contingency; The Coffee Crisis for Conventional Small-Scale Coffee Farmers in Brazil. *The Geographical Journal* 174 (3): 223 – 234.

Watt, K.S. (1937) African Coffee. *Journal of Royal Africa Society* 36 (143): 194 – 200.

Wood, A.P. (1983) The Decline of Seasonal Migration to the South – West Ethiopia. *Journals of Geographical Association* 68 (1): 53 – 56.